Science at the Edge

In Vitro Fertilization

KT-529-770

Ann Fullick

Heinemann
LIBRARY

www.heinemann.co.uk/library
Visit our website to find out more information about **Heinemann Library** books.

To order:
☎ Phone 44 (0) 1865 888066
🖹 Send a fax to 44 (0) 1865 314091
💻 Visit the Heinemann Bookshop at www.heinemann.co.uk/library to browse our catalogue and order online.

First published in Great Britain by Heinemann Library, Halley Court, Jordan Hill, Oxford OX2 8EJ, a division of Reed Educational and Professional Publishing Ltd. Heinemann is a registered trademark of Reed Educational and Professional Publishing Ltd.

OXFORD MELBOURNE AUCKLAND JOHANNESBURG BLANTYRE
GABORONE IBADAN PORTSMOUTH NH (USA) CHICAGO

Designed by Tinstar Design (www.tinstar.co.uk)
Illustrations by Art Construction
Originated by Ambassador Litho Ltd.
Printed and bound in Hong Kong/China

ISBN 0 431 14881 3
06 05 04 03 02
10 9 8 7 6 5 4 3 2 1

British Library Cataloguing in Publication Data
Fullick, Ann
      In vitro fertilization. – (Science at the edge)
      1.Fertilization in vitro, Human – Juvenile literature
      2.Fertilization in vitro, Human – Moral and ethical aspects – Juvenile Literature
      I.Title
      618.1'78'059

Acknowledgements
The Publisher would like to thank the following for permission to reproduce photographs: Corbis: Anna Palmer p9, Scott T. Smith p53; Associated Press: p51; Bubbles: Jonathan Chappell p10; Camera Press: p17; CARE at the Park Hospital: p39; Doriver Lilley: pp36, 41; Mary Evans Picture Library: p18; Medipics: Dan McCoy 27; Michael Dooley: p33; PA Photos: pp32, 54; Popperfoto: p23, 43; Rex Features: p22; Sally and Richard Greenhill: p12; Science Photo Library: pp4, 7, 13, 14, 25, 28, 34, 44, 48, 55, 56, Dr Yorgos Nikas p21; The Wellcome Trust Photo Library: p26; Topham Picturepoint: pp35, 49, Press Association p57; Tudor Photography: p30.

Cover photograph reproduced with permission of Science Photo Library.

Thanks for their invaluable input to Doriver and Ian Lilley, Nicola Monks, Michael Dooley and Pip Scorey.

Every effort has been made to contact copyright holders of any material reproduced in this book. Any omissions will be rectified in subsequent printings if notice is given to the Publisher.

Disclaimer
All the Internet addresses (URLs) given in this book were valid at the time of going to press. However, due to the dynamic nature of the Internet, some addresses may have changed, or sites may have changed or ceased to exist since publication. While the author and Publisher regret any inconvenience this may cause readers, no responsibility for any such changes can be accepted by either the author or the Publisher.

Any words appearing in the text in bold, **like this**, are explained in the Glossary.

Contents

An everyday miracle?   4

What causes infertility?   10

Treating infertility without IVF   16

The IVF story   18

How does IVF work?   24

The price of success   32

Doriver's story   36

Beyond IVF   42

Ethics, issues and the law   46

Where do we go from here?   54

Timeline   58

Glossary   60

Sources of information   63

Index   64

An everyday miracle?

Every moment of every day a baby is born somewhere around the world. Each new human being comes into existence as the result of the joining of two minute cells from the parents to form a single new cell. It is this cell which then grows and divides to form the billions of cells that make up the body of a newborn baby.

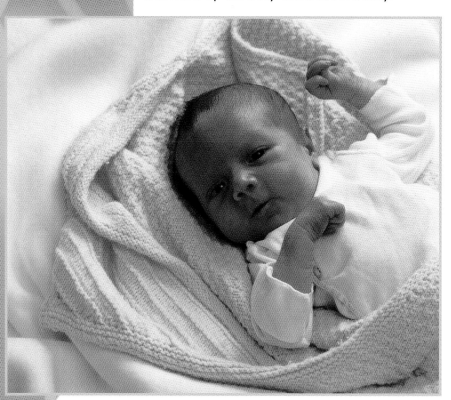

Although it happens every day, the safe arrival of a baby – which has grown over the course of nine months from a single fertilized human egg cell – is still an amazing event.

Infertility

For lots of people, having babies is very easy. There is a time each month when, if the couple make love, there is a chance that an **ovum** (egg) in the body of the woman will be **fertilized** by a **sperm** from the man and nine months later a new baby will be born. In fact many people spend years trying to avoid pregnancy, using different methods

of **contraception** to make sure that sperm and eggs don't meet. But what happens if pregnancy and babies don't happen when they *are* wanted?

Infertility has always been an issue – King Henry VIII got rid of several wives who could not produce him the son and heir he so desperately wanted! The lives of many ordinary people have also been blighted by the inability to have a much-wanted child. Although there are many different causes of infertility, for centuries the solutions were few and far between – adopting a child or becoming resigned to childlessness were the main options.

> '*Not being able to have a baby of your own is the most heart-breaking experience.*'
>
> Jilly Cooper, journalist and writer

So what can we do about it today? In the last 50 years, it has become increasingly possible to treat and overcome at least some forms of infertility. A wide variety of options are now available for couples who cannot produce a child naturally. These range from simple tests that make it possible to pinpoint when a woman is most likely to get pregnant, to complex techniques such as *in vitro* fertilization or IVF. This is a form of treatment where an egg and sperm are brought together outside the mother's body. They are usually mixed in a glass **Petri dish**, hence the name *in vitro* fertilization – *in vitro* is Latin for 'in glass'. The developing **embryo** is then replaced into the mother's body. The development of IVF has resulted in the births of thousands of babies around the world to people who would otherwise have had no hope of becoming pregnant. And IVF has led the way for the development of other methods to help couples have babies. These even include injecting a single sperm into an egg before replacing it in the mother's body.

Like most scientific breakthroughs, our increased ability to control human **fertility** is something of a mixed blessing. It can bring great personal happiness to couples who would otherwise be unable to have a child. At the same time it also opens up many questions about embryos which are created and then not needed, and the possibilities for changing the inherited material of an embryo before it is returned to the mother. As new and ever more sophisticated treatments for infertility are discovered, the **ethics** of each need to be discussed. Yet the driving force behind the whole technology remains the desperate desire of infertile couples to have a child of their own.

The biology of reproduction

Young children cannot have children of their own, but as we grow and mature the parts of the body involved in making babies – technically known as **reproduction** – become active. These include the sexual organs and a gland in the brain. For many people these systems start up and run fairly smoothly, but for a growing number, things don't quite work as they should. So how does the body of a healthy, fertile woman or man work?

The fertile female

For about two days in every month a woman is fertile – she has produced an egg that is mature and ready to meet a sperm. The events leading up to and following this special time form a 28-day cycle of fertility, called the **menstrual cycle**.

Inside the body of every newborn baby girl are the eggs (called ova) that will form her future children. Once the girl goes through **puberty** the **ovaries**, which contain the eggs, become active in response to chemical signals called **hormones**.

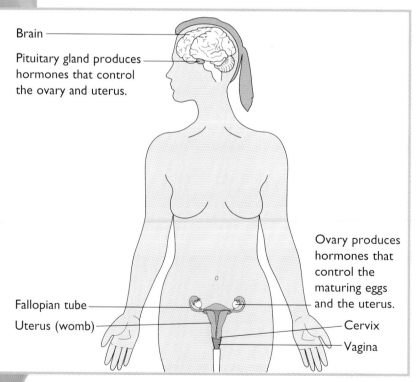

Brain

Pituitary gland produces hormones that control the ovary and uterus.

Ovary produces hormones that control the maturing eggs and the uterus.

Fallopian tube

Uterus (womb)

Cervix

Vagina

A delicate balance of hormones controls the reproductive system in a woman.

Follicle Stimulating Hormone (FSH) is made by the **pituitary gland** in the brain and it has a direct effect on the ovaries. It makes some of the eggs grow and mature, ready for release. FSH also makes the ovary produce another female hormone, **oestrogen**. This triggers the build-up of the lining of the **uterus** (the organ in which the baby grows and develops) ready to nurture a pregnancy. After about fourteen days an egg is released – this is known as **ovulation** – and it leaves the ovary. The egg travels through the **Fallopian tube** towards the uterus. If it meets some sperm on the way up, it may be fertilized and a pregnancy begins. If not, the lining of the uterus gradually breaks down and passes out of the body. This is called menstruation.

Reproduction in the male

Men do not have a reproductive cycle as women do, but they do have male reproductive hormones produced by the pituitary gland and by the male sex organs, the **testes**. In response to these hormones the testes make a constant supply of sperm, and other glands make the various secretions which are mixed with the sperm to form **semen**.

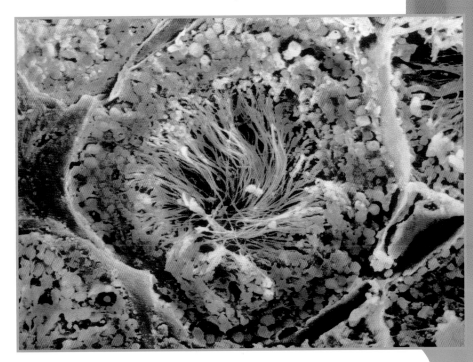

Whereas women usually produce a single mature egg each month, millions of sperm are produced all the time in the testes. The tails of hundreds of developing sperm can be seen here, in a tiny tube in the testes.

From conception to birth

Once a couple decide that they want a baby they need to try and make sure that sperm are present when a mature egg is released from the woman's ovary. Every time they make love the man releases semen containing millions of sperm into the woman's vagina. At around the same time, if the woman is at the fertile point in her menstrual cycle, an egg will be released from the ovary and begin its journey along the Fallopian tube. How do the egg and the sperm meet?

The egg cannot move – it is wafted along the Fallopian tube by the beating of millions of tiny hair-like cilia which move it slowly away from the ovary towards the uterus. After ovulation the egg only lives for around 48 hours.

The sperm, on the other hand, have an enormously long journey to make as they travel through **mucus** and other secretions in the vagina and **cervix**, up through the uterus and on into the Fallopian tube which contains the egg. The journey of a single sperm can be compared to a person setting off from Britain and swimming to the USA – through treacle!

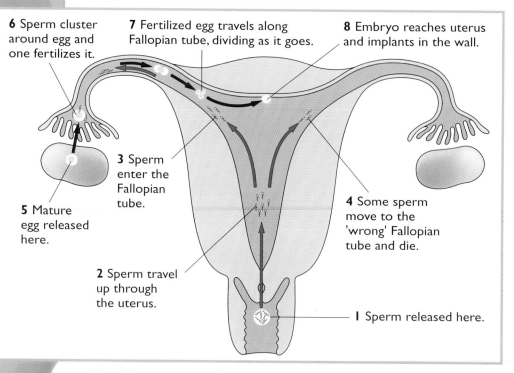

6 Sperm cluster around egg and one fertilizes it.

7 Fertilized egg travels along Fallopian tube, dividing as it goes.

8 Embryo reaches uterus and implants in the wall.

3 Sperm enter the Fallopian tube.

5 Mature egg released here.

4 Some sperm move to the 'wrong' Fallopian tube and die.

2 Sperm travel up through the uterus.

1 Sperm released here.

The Fallopian tubes are the site where the egg and the sperm meet at fertilization, and where the first divisions of the newly formed embryo take place.

Each sperm makes frantic lashing movements with its tail, which keep it suspended in the liquids, and it is moved to the egg by natural muscle movements of the uterus. Some sperm reach the Fallopian tubes very quickly – in a matter of minutes – but millions are lost along the way. This is why so many sperm are produced in the first place, because the odds against any of them reaching the egg are so high!

Fertilization

Once the sperm reach the egg, how is the egg actually fertilized? The sperm cluster round the egg, attracted by chemical messages it sends out. Special digestive **enzymes** in the head of the sperm act to dissolve away the protective jelly coating of the egg. Finally one sperm manages to break through and get inside the egg – after that no other sperm can get in. The **nucleus** of the sperm contains **genetic** information from the man while the nucleus of the egg contains genetic information from the woman. Once they fuse together, fertilization has taken place – a new genetic individual is formed and a potential new life has begun!

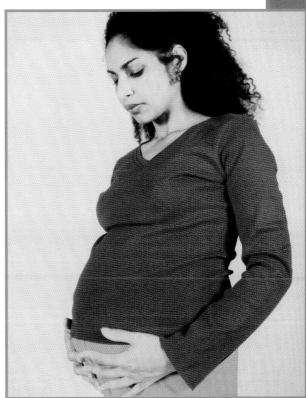

After fertilization the single cell begins to grow and divide as it continues to travel along the Fallopian tube to the uterus. By the time it reaches the uterus it is a small ball of cells ready to implant in the blood-rich lining that has developed in order to support it.

Once the fertilized egg has implanted in the uterus, cell divisions, the specialization of tissue and lots of growth take place. After nine months, a fully formed baby human being is ready to emerge and take a place in the world.

What causes infertility?

When a couple decide that they want to start a family and begin to try to have a baby, most expect to get pregnant straight away. After all, many of them have spent years trying very hard not to get pregnant by mistake! Even if a young, **fertile** couple have unprotected intercourse at the right stage of the monthly cycle there is no guarantee that they will become pregnant. The percentage chance that they will conceive gets steadily lower as they get older, and it is also reduced by lifestyle factors such as smoking, drinking and being overweight.

For an increasing number of couples, the months without a positive pregnancy test turn into years. When **infertility** seems to be staring people in the face, it becomes very important to understand why pregnancy is not happening, and what, if anything, can be done about it.

When pregnancy doesn't happen, every monthly **period** comes as a bitter disappointment. Even children's clothes in a shop window can make it seem as if everyone else has a baby.

Whose problem?

It is almost inevitable that, if a couple cannot have a child, they wonder whose 'fault' it is. For centuries it was assumed that childlessness was the woman's fault. We now know better! Failing to get pregnant can be the result of problems in either partner, or even both.

In about a third of all cases of infertility there is indeed a problem in the way that the body of the woman is working. However, in over a third of the cases, it is the reproductive system of the man which is not functioning as it should. The final group of infertility cases are either the result of both the man and the woman in a couple being a bit less fertile than normal or – the most puzzling of all – both partners are theoretically healthy but pregnancy just doesn't happen.

Finding out

IVF has been successful in helping to overcome some forms of infertility, but it is still a very specialized area of medicine. A couple who are having problems in conceiving a baby do not start their quest for a child with the IVF specialist – they begin with the family doctor.

Typically a doctor will check the general health of the couple in case there are any other causes of infertility not related to their reproductive systems. The doctor will also check that the woman is not taking the **contraceptive** pill and whether the couple are having sexual intercourse at the time of the month when the woman is most fertile. Another check will be on any other medications either partner may be taking, and whether either of them smoke or drink. Sometimes this allows the doctors to find a simple solution to fertility problems so that medical intervention is not needed to start a family.

For many the solution is not quite so simple, and doctors will refer a couple to an infertility specialist when it becomes apparent that they are having real difficulty in conceiving. For older couples, especially, the 'biological clock' is ticking away fast, as a woman's fertility begins to fall as she approaches 40. It is important that they start working with an infertility specialist as soon as possible. However, most specialists would rather see all couples with fertility problems sooner rather than later, to try and find a successful solution to their problems.

An infertile woman...

When a couple can't have a baby a number of different tests are carried out on both partners to try and find out the cause of the infertility, because different causes need different solutions.

Ovulation problems

To find out why a woman is not conceiving, doctors look for both physical and chemical causes. One of the first checks will be to see if **ovulation** is occurring – because no egg equals no baby!

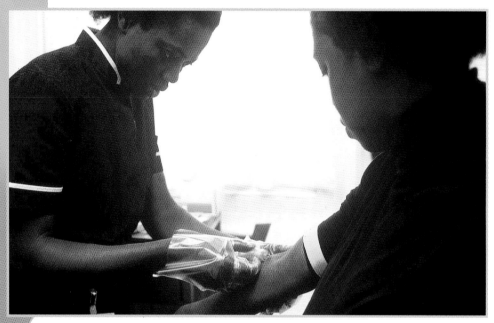

By measuring the levels of different hormones in the blood, doctors can build up a pretty good picture of what is going on and whether ovulation is taking place.

'It is estimated that problems with ovulation occur in 25 per cent of infertile couples. This is an important problem to identify, as most of these patients can be treated successfully.'

Susan Smith, Deputy Medical Director, Bridge Fertility Centre

There can be several explanations for a lack of ovulation. Sometimes the situation is very stark – there are no eggs in the **ovaries**. However, this is relatively rare and is the cause of infertility in only one to two per cent of the women who have difficulty in conceiving. If there are no eggs then the woman will never conceive naturally. IVF can help provide her only chance of motherhood. Some women who have had families of their own are prepared to act as egg **donors**. This means they allow eggs to be collected from their ovaries and given to other, infertile women. A donated egg can be **fertilized** by **sperm** from the man and placed in the infertile woman's body to develop.

However, in many women who do not ovulate the cause is easier to deal with. Some women don't make enough **FSH** to stimulate the release of the mature eggs from the ovary and others don't make any at all. Synthetic (laboratory-created) **hormones** can be used that will replace natural FSH, bringing about ovulation and so, hopefully, pregnancy (see page 16).

Tangled tubes?

The most common female physical problem preventing pregnancy is that the **Fallopian tubes** are twisted, scarred or blocked in some way. The Fallopian tubes are inside the body, hidden to human eyes. About 11cm long, they lead from the ovaries to the **uterus**. If the tubes are damaged, this prevents the sperm from meeting the egg and even more importantly, stops the egg, fertilized or not, from travelling along to the uterus. Thirty per cent of female infertility is the result of damaged Fallopian tubes.

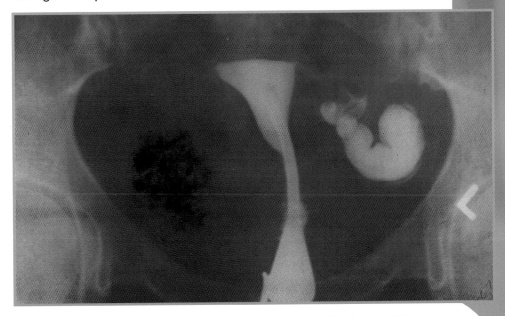

Techniques like this hysterosalpingogram help doctors decide whether IVF is necessary – if the Fallopian tubes are damaged, as these are, a normal **conception** is impossible. The uterus is the pale, triangular shape in the centre. The Fallopian tube on the left of the picture is not visible meaning that no dye has passed into it from the uterus. This shows that it is blocked. The tube on the right is damaged.

Damage to the tubes is revealed during an investigation known as a **laparoscopy**, usually combined with a dye test. During a laparoscopy a fine telescope is inserted into the abdominal cavity so doctors can look at the Fallopian tubes from the outside. Not surprisingly the woman is given a general anaesthetic so that she is unconscious during this procedure. For the dye test, a coloured dye is injected through the **cervix** and the doctors watch to see how the dye progresses through the Fallopian tubes – if the tubes are clear, the dye will spill out of the ends of them. These tests give a good first idea of whether or not the tubes are blocked or if there are any abnormalities in the uterus itself. If there seem to be problems the investigation can be taken further with a hysterosalpingogram. For this a special dye that shows up on X-rays is injected up into the cervix. The dye shows up blockages in the Fallopian tubes on the X-rays that are taken.

Sometimes a technique that involves tiny instruments placed into the Fallopian tubes can be used to try and reopen them, but the technique itself can damage the very delicate tubes. When the tubes are badly damaged or blocked then the only hope of a solution is IVF.

... or an infertile man

When a couple visit their doctor about fertility problems, investigations will be made into the fertility of the man as well as the woman. There are two crucial factors. Is the man producing sperm in his **semen**, and are they normal, healthy and active? The answer to both of these questions comes from a careful examination of the man's semen.

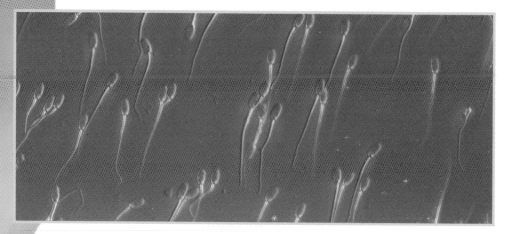

Using a microscope to view a fresh sample of semen reveals just what state the sperm are in, and how many of them there are.

In normal healthy semen there will be hundreds of millions of sperm. In fact the lowest number of sperm counted as normal is 20 million sperm per 1 cm³ of semen! Once the sperm count falls below this level it begins to affect fertility – remember that only one out of every 2000 sperm will make it from the cervix to the Fallopian tubes. If the sperm count is just a bit below normal there are certain things that the man can do to increase the numbers – all of them very low tech! If the **testes** get too warm, the level of sperm production falls, so cool showers or baths, baggy underwear and loose clothing can help to increase the sperm count. Smoking and drinking alcohol are known to lower the sperm count, so reducing or stopping these habits can also help increase sperm numbers. If the count is really low, it gets more difficult.

Numbers aren't everything

The overall sperm count is important, but the ability of sperm to fertilize eggs successfully depends on more than numbers. The motility of the sperm is very important too – in other words, how active are they and how well do they swim? For the man to be fertile his sperm need to have actively lashing tails and around 50 per cent of them must swim forward in straight lines rather than round and round in circles.

Even if a man has lots of active sperm it isn't quite enough to be sure that he is fertile. It is also very important that the semen doesn't contain too many abnormal sperm. Every man produces a certain number of sperm with two heads instead of one, or with two tails, or broken necks. But if the percentage of these abnormal sperm gets too high, then the chances of a successful pregnancy fall.

Overcoming male infertility is not easy. Until recently the best hope was for the woman to be treated with healthy sperm given by an unknown donor, often mixed with some of her partner's sperm. However, some of the latest developments of IVF involve using a single normal sperm and injecting it into the woman's egg cell which is then implanted in her uterus. This exciting new development is leading to potential treatment for almost all men with fertility problems, as the numbers of men who produce no healthy sperm at all is relatively small.

'There are very few cases of male infertility or sub-fertility that can actually be cured. Generally when we refer to treatment we mean techniques that enable us to **circumvent** the problem.'

Sue Avery, Scientific Director, Bourn Hall Clinic

Treating infertility without IVF

The best known treatment for **infertility** is, without a doubt, IVF. It is never far away from the news headlines, not least because of the many new treatments that have followed in its wake. But when a couple first have **fertility** problems, the way they are treated will not always involve IVF.

Smoking, drinking alcohol, being very overweight or underweight, eating an unhealthy diet or having a lack of folic acid (a type of vitamin B) in the diet can make it difficult or impossible to conceive. For a surprising number of people, simples changes in lifestyle can make **conception** possible and result in the birth of a baby.

> 'Without very overweight or very underweight patients –
> in other words, if everyone was within the ideal weight
> range – the number of patients in my infertility clinic
> would be significantly reduced.'
>
> Mr Michael Dooley, Consultant,
> Winterbourne Hospital Infertility Clinic

One of the most common ways of treating fertility problems involves **fertility drugs**. These are not only remarkably successful in their own right, but have also paved the way for the development of IVF. One of the main reasons women fail to get pregnant is because they do not produce mature eggs. Fertility drugs are chemicals that work in different ways to stimulate the woman's body to produce and release a mature egg from the **ovary**.

The most widely used drug is clomiphene citrate. This drug works by fooling the body into making extra **FSH** and so stimulating the production of eggs by the ovaries. When women do not make any of their own FSH they can be given different drugs which actually contain human **hormones**. These stimulate the ovaries directly. Other fertility drugs can be used if the mature eggs are not released from the ovaries.

The use of these drugs has been very successful in helping many infertile couples to have children, and it has been vital in the development of IVF. To carry out this technique doctors need to harvest a number of eggs to **fertilize** outside the body. Even with fertile women, only one or at most two eggs mature enough each month to be released from the ovary. So when doctors are working with their patients towards IVF, fertility drugs are an important part of the preparation.

Three's a crowd?

Fertility drugs have helped many infertile couples to have children, but when they were first developed they caused problems of their own. In the early days of fertility drugs, doctors were not always sure of the doses to use, and many of the women using the drugs had multiple pregnancies – in other words, more than one egg was released and fertilized at the same time. Twins did not cause too many problems, but far more people than expected had triplets, quads or even more babies.

Large multiple pregnancies cause many problems. When lots of babies develop in the same **uterus**, there is a much increased risk that labour will start very early as the uterus becomes hopelessly overstretched. And very tiny babies, born at this stage, are quite likely to die or become brain damaged. Now, with increased knowledge of the way fertility drugs work and close control of the dosage, large multiple pregnancies can usually be avoided.

It would be easy to think that someone desperate for a baby would welcome an instant family of three, four or more children, but it is not quite that simple. If lots of babies arrive at once the demands on the parents, physically, mentally and financially, can be enormous.

The IVF story

For centuries people have tried to overcome **infertility** by whatever means they had available. Scientists and doctors have trodden a long and difficult path to reach the stage we are at today, with IVF and other treatments holding out the hope of a baby to many who would otherwise be childless. Many aspects of human **fertility** had to be understood before it became possible to **fertilize** a human egg outside of the mother's body and return it to her **uterus** to grow into a full-term, healthy baby.

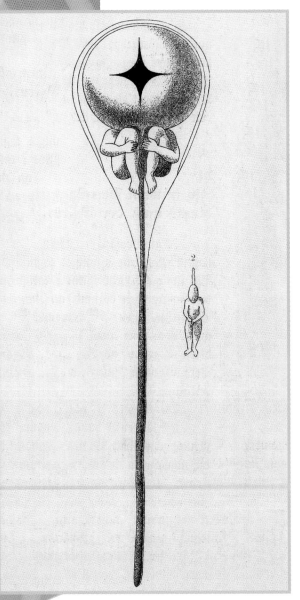

Exploring ways of treating infertility is not new science. In the 3rd century, Jewish thinkers were discussing whether it was possible for people to become pregnant by accidental **artificial insemination**. By the 14th century, Arabs were using artificial insemination in their horse-breeding programmes. In 1777 an Italian priest began

For many years people had little understanding of how human reproduction worked – for example, a long-held belief was that the man supplied the entire new baby in his sperm, and the woman simply acted as a kind of 'super-seedbed', providing the growing child with all that it needed until it was born. Until beliefs like this were overturned by scientific knowledge, any attempts to overcome infertility were doomed to fail.

experiments with artificial insemination in reptiles, and in 1785 there was a major breakthrough, when John Hunter, a Scottish surgeon, made his first attempts at human artificial insemination. As a result of his experiments a child was born that same year.

Into the 20th century

The 20th century saw many significant advances in the treatment of infertility. In the early years of the century scientists like the Americans Samuel Crowe, Harvey Cushing and John Homans began to unravel the complex chemical control of human fertility. They, along with other scientists, discovered, isolated and identified the **hormones** made by the **pituitary gland** in the brain, and by the **ovaries** and **testes**.

Towards the end of the 20th century there was a great deal of controversy and debate about IVF and some of the other treatments which have developed from it. However, this sort of debate is nothing new. Assisting couples to have babies using artificial means has always raised strong feelings – even in the early days there were people who were unhappy at what they saw as unnatural interference with nature.

When early reports of artificial insemination using **sperm** from a **donor** were published in the *British Medical Journal* in 1945 there was great debate in the British Parliament. At that time British researchers were the leaders in the field. In 1948, the Archbishop of Canterbury, the most senior clergyman in Britain, recommended that the practice should be made a criminal offence. The government didn't follow that recommendation, although they did say that the practice was 'undesirable and not to be encouraged'.

In 1949, an Italian, Dr Piero Donini, produced the first human **fertility drug**, but it took many years – until 1962 – before the first baby was born as a result of drug-triggered **ovulation**. Meanwhile, in 1954, things had moved forward again: there was a report of four successful pregnancies following the use of frozen sperm. In spite of this, it was another sixteen years – that is until 1970 – before the use of artificial insemination using donor sperm became an officially accepted treatment for infertility in the UK. By this time the research had spread across the world, and in many countries, including the USA, Australia and parts of Europe, artificial insemination was accepted and used.

Understanding grows

As the 1960s dawned, doctors and scientists all over the world were learning more and more about different parts of the process of **reproduction**, and all of this knowledge and understanding was needed before IVF could be developed.

Their knowledge included the use of fertility drugs to regulate the numbers of eggs that matured in the ovary. Developments in the understanding of the ways in which eggs mature and the events of ovulation were also important. As scientists moved closer towards IVF, it became vitally important that the process of fertilization was thoroughly understood. Just as vital was knowledge about the way early human **embryos** develop *in vitro*, outside of their natural environment in the body of the mother. It soon became apparent that human embryos could not survive long outside the ideal environment of the mother, and so transfer back to the mother would need to be done within the first few days of fertilization.

Only once all of this knowledge and understanding was in place could scientists take the next steps forward and move towards developing IVF.

The early development of the human embryo

How does an embryo develop? Once an egg and a sperm have joined, the two **nuclei** fuse together. This means that the **genetic** material of the father is combined with the genetic material of the mother. Once this has happened a new cell with a unique combination of **DNA** has formed. Immediately the cell begins to divide, and about 30 hours after fertilization the developing embryo has two cells. After 40–50 hours each of these two cells has also divided in two and the embryo consists of four cells. In the human body, these divisions take place as the fertilized egg is beginning to move down the **Fallopian tube**. Cell divisions continue, until there are sixteen cells. Eventually, about four to five days after fertilization, a hollow ball of around 80 cells arrives in the uterus, where it implants itself. At this stage the embryo is known as a **blastocyst**. The developing embryo in IVF may be returned to the body of the mother at any stage, from two cells to blastocyst. From then on, the remaining stages of development will take place in the protected environment of her uterus.

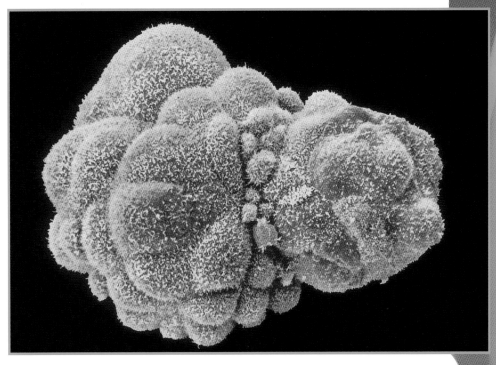

Increasingly, IVF clinics are returning the developing embryo to the uterus at the blastocyst stage rather than at an earlier stage, because this is the point that the embryo would naturally arrive in the uterus and implant.

Enter Edwards and Steptoe

The first time a human egg was fertilized successfully outside of the female body was in 1969. It was achieved by Dr Robert Edwards, an academic **physiologist** working at Cambridge University in the UK. He used human ovaries that had been removed during surgery as the source of the eggs. The eggs needed to be kept in a very special, chemically balanced fluid – they couldn't just be taken out of the body and left in a dish. This first human *in vitro* fertilization took place in a culture medium, which is a mixture of chemicals and water used to culture eggs and developing embryos. This had been used very successfully for the *in vitro* fertilization of hamster eggs during earlier, animal-based research into infertility treatments.

At the same time, Mr Patrick Steptoe, a **gynaecologist** working at the Royal Oldham Hospital, was developing methods of extracting mature human eggs from the ovary by **laparoscopy**. He could 'harvest' eggs, sucking them up from the ripe **follicle** (cell surrounding the egg) at the stage when they could be fertilized. This was brave stuff, because at that time laparoscopy was considered 'a dangerous procedure'.

The birth of IVF – and Louise Brown

By 1971, Edwards and Steptoe had met and were sharing their ideas and expertise to work towards a successful fertility treatment. They worked on retrieving eggs from volunteers so they could time egg collection to perfection, and on the best culture conditions for maintaining a human egg and an early embryo outside the body – *in vitro*. They did not use fertility drugs to enhance egg development. They simply monitored their patients very carefully and when ovulation appeared imminent (at whatever hour of the day or night) they operated and collected the egg by laparoscopy.

Before long they felt ready to attempt a pregnancy in an infertile volunteer. By 1975, success was on the horizon – a human embryo was replaced successfully in the body of its mother and a pregnancy began. But the excitement was short-lived. The longed-for pregnancy developed not in the uterus of the mother but in her Fallopian tube. This is known as an **ectopic pregnancy**, and it can cause terrible pain and the risk of severe damage or even death to the mother. An operation was carried out to remove the tube, and the embryo with it, dashing the hopes of doctors and scientists alike. It was also a terrible blow to the couple who so desperately wanted a child that they were prepared to act as human guinea pigs in this amazing experiment.

Robert Edwards (on the left) and Patrick Steptoe – the pioneers whose work resulted in the birth of the first IVF baby and gave hope to countless infertile couples.

However, for Edwards and Steptoe success was not far away. They continued their experiments, in spite of growing media pressure and the clamour of groups who were unhappy with their interference in the process of reproduction. In 1977, they removed a single mature egg from the ovary of Lesley Brown, and fertilized it with sperm from her husband. The embryo that resulted was implanted back into Lesley's uterus and to everyone's delight she became pregnant. Finally, on July 25 1978, Louise Brown was born – a healthy baby girl conceived in a glass **Petri dish**. This was truly ground-breaking science – and also the end of years of heartache for the Browns. Both Patrick Steptoe and Robert Edwards were present at the birth – they must have been almost as happy as Mr and Mrs Brown! IVF as a way of overcoming infertility had arrived at last.

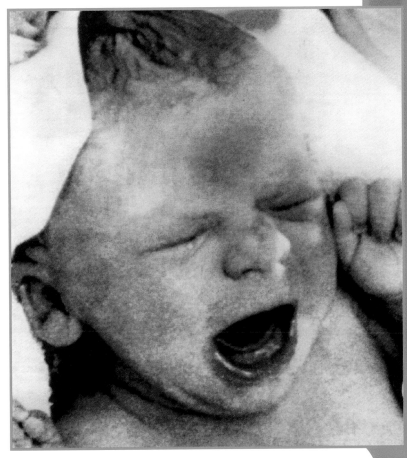

Louise Brown, the first baby born as a result of fertilization outside the body. The media coined the phrase 'test-tube baby' to describe her astonishing **conception**, and this colloquial term for IVF stuck.

How does IVF work?

The birth of Louise Brown in 1978 was the climax of years of research – but it was just the beginning of new **infertility** treatments. In the years since then IVF has continued to develop in quite spectacular fashion – the techniques have been refined and new treatments added. Within two years, two Australian groups of researchers helped couples have babies through IVF, but they used a rather different technique. They stimulated their patients with **fertility drugs** to make sure that plenty of eggs were produced. As they had a higher success rate than the British team, it was their methods of egg collection which were widely adopted. Even Edwards and Steptoe later adopted the use of fertility drugs to stimulate the production of more than one egg, a process known as **superovulation**.

IVF offers a way of overcoming infertility for women whose **Fallopian tubes** are blocked, twisted or damaged beyond repair, where neither eggs nor **sperm** can travel along the tubes. The treatment combines the egg and sperm outside the body, and returns the developing **embryo** to the **uterus**, bypassing the need for the Fallopian tubes.

If a couple who are infertile because of damaged Fallopian tubes decide, in consultation with their doctors, that a course of IVF treatment is the way forward for them, what can they expect?

Setting out

Almost every couple who undergo IVF treatment receive initial counselling. This is to make sure that they realize that although the treatment offers them the hope of a baby, it in no way guarantees one. The chances of a couple actually achieving a successful pregnancy are no higher – and probably lower – than a **fertile** couple attempting to get pregnant by natural methods. If they do get pregnant using IVF, then the risk of multiple pregnancy is higher than for a normal couple. Most clinics feel it is very important that their patients realize these facts before they embark on a course of treatment.

Infertility clinics, such as this one in Milan, Italy, need to find out as much as they can about their patients as quickly as possible, so they use medical notes from the doctors who have carried out earlier investigations into the couple's fertility problem. They also need to talk to the couple to find out what they are looking for and if they are likely to be suitable for the treatments on offer.

IVF clinics vary widely in who they will accept onto their programmes. Couples who seek help are not just those with blocked or damaged Fallopian tubes. Some couples don't get pregnant and there is no clear reason why not. If they have tried all other methods and failed, IVF may offer them a final chance.

Some clinics will only accept younger couples who are more likely to succeed, both to avoid giving false hope to other couples and to keep their 'baby per treatment' average as high as possible. The rate of live babies achieved per treatment is one of the most important factors couples look at when deciding which infertility clinic to choose. Obviously the clinics make their money by treating patients, so the more couples who choose the clinic, the more financially successful it will be.

Other clinics specialize in just those most-difficult-to-treat cases, older couples, couples where both partners have infertility problems and couples who have already had a number of IVF failures. Yet others are relatively unselective. It will depend on many things including the staff running the clinics and how the clinic is funded. In the UK, where the National Health Service (NHS) pays for the infertility treatment of some couples, funding is only made available for couples where there seems, statistically, a good chance of success – and NHS funding is only available in some parts of the country. Patients funding their own treatment may rely less on statistics and more on hope when deciding whether to pay for treatment.

Managing IVF

The first important stage of IVF treatment is to make sure that the woman produces a number of good quality eggs. This is brought about by carefully measured doses of fertility drugs. The development of ripe **follicles** on the surface of the **ovary** is then monitored. If not many follicles are developing, doctors will not try to collect eggs. Instead they will try again during the next **menstrual cycle**, giving the woman a higher dosage of drugs.

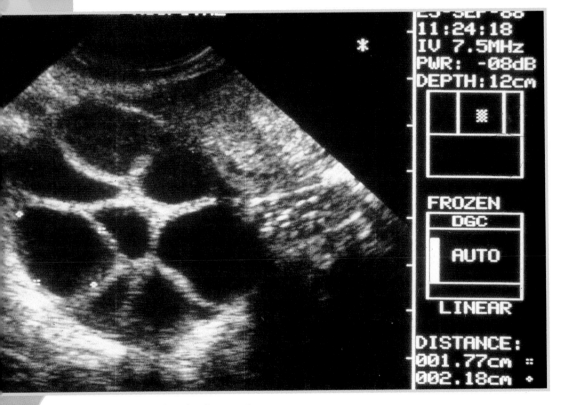

Using ultrasound technology, a doctor can monitor the state of the follicles on the surface of a woman's ovaries without opening up her body.

The development of the eggs maturing in the ovaries is monitored using **ultrasound**, which enables doctors to see how many follicles are forming. Blood tests may also be used to monitor levels of a **hormone** called oestradiol – as the follicles develop, the levels of oestradiol increase. By combining the information from the blood tests and the ultrasound, doctors can build up a very accurate picture of how many eggs are developing in the ovary and when will be the best time to collect them. About 36 hours before the egg collection is due, the woman is given a final injection of yet another hormone, human chorionic gonadotrophin (hCG). This helps to make sure that the eggs are fully mature in their follicles.

Collecting the eggs is another vital and tense stage of the process. If a number of healthy, mature eggs are not collected, the process cannot go ahead. And just because there are ripe follicles in the ovaries this does not necessarily mean the eggs will be collected successfully – harvesting eggs is a tricky and delicate business.

The process is carried out with the woman either sedated or under a general anaesthetic. An ultrasound probe is placed inside the vagina because this gives a better picture of the position of the ripe follicles than a probe on the stomach. A needle is carefully guided through the wall of the vagina into the body cavity next to the ovaries. The point is then carefully manoeuvred into a ripe follicle. The liquid inside the follicle, including the mature egg, is sucked up into a tube connected to a small pot to collect the eggs.

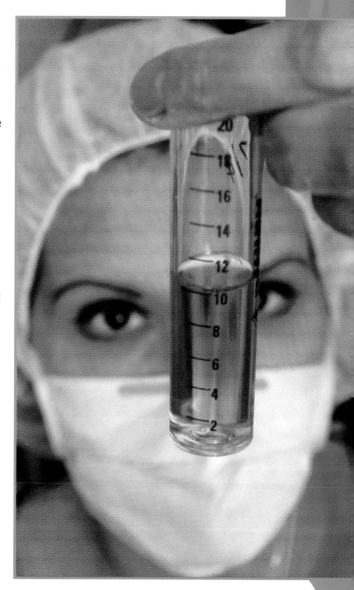

Success! For an infertile couple, even the successful collection of a number of mature eggs is a big step forward. They are held here in culture.

The big moment

Once the eggs have been collected from the woman they are placed in a special liquid that mimics the normal body fluids. Each egg is put into a small dish in an incubator and kept at body temperature. The acidity level (the pH) is also kept the same as the normal body fluids. This is very important so that the eggs continue to develop properly. The male partner then produces some **semen**, from which samples of very active sperm are taken. These are added to the dishes containing the eggs four to six hours after the eggs were collected – at the time they would naturally have been released from the ovary – and if all goes well with the insemination the process of **fertilization** begins. This takes about eighteen hours from start to finish and it is then another twelve hours before the first cell division takes place. At this stage a couple will find out if they have actually achieved any embryos.

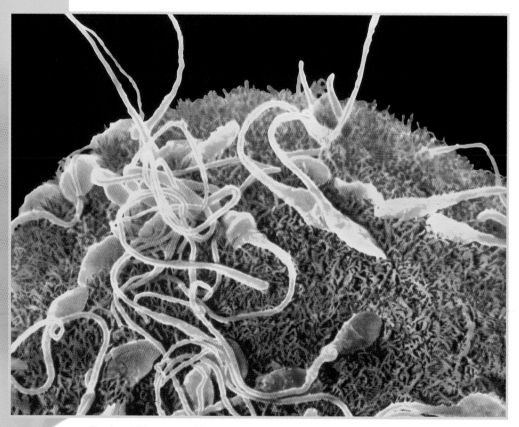

During IVF we are able to see the actual process of fertilization, that would otherwise be hidden within the Fallopian tubes of a woman's body. The availability of the very early embryo means it can be checked for serious **genetic** abnormalities before it is replaced in the body of the mother.

The dividing of these embryonic cells continues for several days. After two days they contain four cells, after three days there are eight cells and after five days the embryo is a hollow ball of cells called a **blastocyst**. The embryo can be transferred to the woman's body at any of these stages. During this time the health of the minute embryos will be monitored closely by the **embryologist**. Great care is taken that only healthy, undamaged embryos are replaced in the mother's body, and so the dividing cells are regularly observed through a microscope.

'We choose which embryos to replace by looking at their appearance. A good embryo has even cell divisions and the cells aren't forming small fragments. We have a grading system, and the best grades of embryo give the best pregnancy rates. Having said that, we sometimes have embryos with a poor appearance giving rise to healthy pregnancies and equally some beautiful embryos which don't result in pregnancy at all.'

Nicola Monk, embryologist,
Winterbourne Hospital Infertility Clinic

Embryo transfer

In some ways transferring the embryos to the mother's body is the simplest part of the procedure. The hormonal state of the woman's body a few days after **ovulation** means she is ready to receive an embryo. Some embryos – usually two or three – are placed in a very fine tube called a catheter, which is passed up through the woman's **cervix** to the top of the uterus. This is the normal – and ideal – site for the embryo to implant. The tiny balls of cells are deposited here in the uterus. To help improve the chances of pregnancy occurring, many women are given additional treatment with the hormone **progesterone** after the embryos have been replaced in their body.

At this stage the woman can go home and carry on with her ordinary life. It must be very tempting to simply stay in bed and not move, to try and make sure that the tiny embryos stay where they are meant to be! However, all the research shows that this doesn't make the slightest difference to whether the embryos implant or not. After all, an embryo normally manages to implant whatever is going on in the life of its mother!

Finding out

For an infertile couple, the two weeks immediately following embryo transfer must seem never-ending. They have to wait until the woman would be due to have a **period** before they find out if she is actually pregnant or not. Of course, if her period starts, then the IVF has obviously not worked. But if the monthly bleeding does not start on the day it is expected then a very sensitive early pregnancy test can show what is happening to the hormones in the body and give either good news or bad.

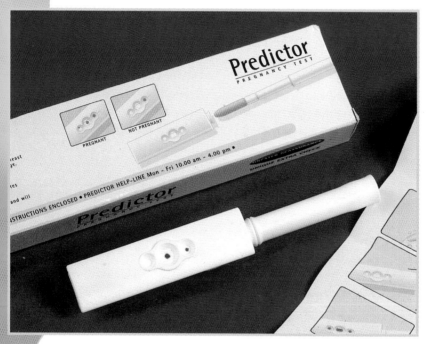

This is the sight that everyone on an IVF programme longs to see. A positive pregnancy test means at least one embryo has implanted and a pregnancy has begun!

An ultrasound scan carried out four to six weeks after the embryos are transferred will confirm the successful pregnancy and also give the couple their first glimpse of their longed-for child – or children! This scan provides important information for the IVF team – it shows them if they have definitely been successful and how many babies are expected. It is also enormously important for the couple concerned, who may well find it very hard to accept the fact that they really are pregnant after trying for so long. Seeing a tiny blob, or blobs, on the ultrasound screen, and the beating of a tiny heart, can help to make the situation seem more real.

Once an IVF pregnancy has been established, it becomes just like any other pregnancy. The worries and fears that every mother has for her unborn child may well be greater in a couple who have tried desperately for years to become pregnant, but the actual risks are no higher – unless of course they are expecting twins or triplets. Even then, the risks of problems developing in the pregnancy are no worse than for anyone else expecting more than one baby to arrive.

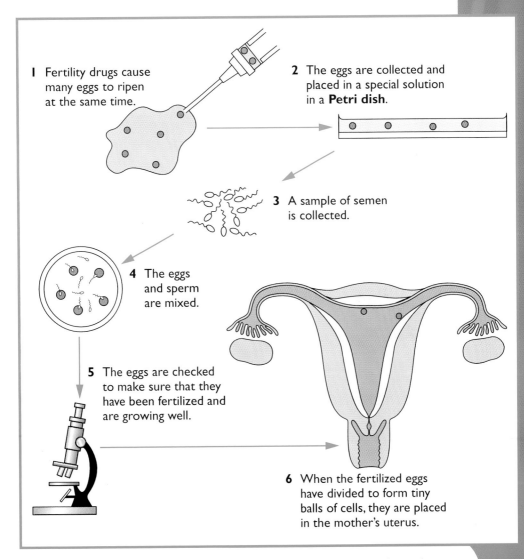

1 Fertility drugs cause many eggs to ripen at the same time.

2 The eggs are collected and placed in a special solution in a **Petri dish**.

3 A sample of semen is collected.

4 The eggs and sperm are mixed.

5 The eggs are checked to make sure that they have been fertilized and are growing well.

6 When the fertilized eggs have divided to form tiny balls of cells, they are placed in the mother's uterus.

The stages in the process of IVF can be summarized in a diagram like this. It makes it all look so simple, and yet the technology used here has taken years to perfect and it is still a long way from guaranteeing that a successful pregnancy will result.

The price of success

IVF is a technique which has improved the chances of having a baby for **infertile** couples all over the world. Thousands and thousands of children have been born as a result of this still relatively new technology. From an initial success rate of well below five per cent, couples now have a 20–25 per cent chance of pregnancy when they undergo IVF. The success rate varies according to the clinical problem as well as the age of the woman. This sounds low but it is similar to the chances of a **fertile** couple achieving a successful pregnancy if they make love at the fertile time of the month.

These are just some of the tens of thousands of children who would not have been born without the technique of IVF.

A clinic lottery?

The chances of success vary greatly from clinic to clinic. Some clinics appear far better at producing live babies as a result of a single treatment than others. When people (or a state, in the case of the UK's National Health Service) are spending large sums of money on treatments for infertility, they have a right to know that they are getting good value for money. Yet raw figures of babies born per treatment can be deceptive and people need to look carefully before making judgements – or choices.

For example, some clinics treat more patients with difficult problems than others. Some clinics specialize in the treatment of older women, or in using **donor** eggs, for which the chances of success are lower than for other IVF treatments. Yet another important factor affecting success rates is the number of **embryos** transferred into the body of the woman, which varies from clinic to clinic. The more embryos that are transferred, the greater the chance of multiple pregnancies. Multiple pregnancies – twins, triplets or more – are known to increase the risk of things going wrong. Triplets and even higher numbers of babies put an immense strain on the body of the mother when she is carrying them, and they are also very difficult for parents to cope with when they are born. The physical and emotional demands of several babies – and the children they grow into – can be very hard to meet without lots of extra support. Yet if one or more of the embryos that has been implanted does not grow to form a baby some parents grieve for the potential babies they have lost.

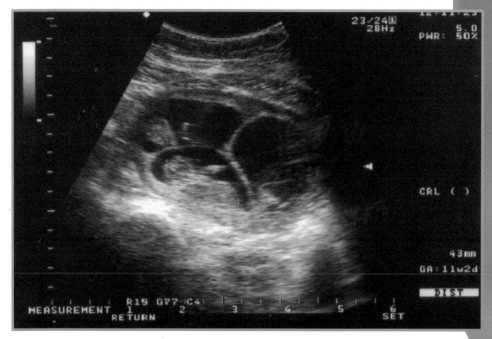

If more than one of the embryos transferred back to the mother's body implants successfully then a multiple pregnancy results. After no babies at all, triplets, shown here, might sound exciting at first, but the reality can be very tough.

'The scan showed twins ... I must admit I felt sad for my other little embryo and wondered where he had gone.'
IVF mother who had three embryos transferred and gave birth to twins

If three or more babies arrive at once, there is the considerable financial pressure of buying food, clothing and everything else for a very large family. So if the number of embryos transferred is not carefully managed, the longed-for arrival of children to an infertile couple can put an almost unbearable strain on them, particularly as they may well have spent much of their savings on infertility treatment. However, if clinics transferred only one embryo to reduce the risk of a multiple pregnancy, they would also reduce the likelihood of pregnancy. **Pros and cons** such as these need to be weighed up carefully when couples and their doctors are deciding how to proceed with treatment. Most centres prefer to implant at least two, but no more than three, embryos at any one time, to strike the best balance between giving a good chance of pregnancy with the least risk of a large multiple birth. In the UK, under the regulations of the Human Fertilisation and Embryology Authority (HFEA), three is the maximum number of embryos which can be transplanted at any one time, but a recent recommendation (2001) is to only replace two.

A frozen harvest

The number of embryos to implant is not the only dilemma facing IVF specialists and their patients. The production of more embryos than are needed for any one transfer means there are other ethical questions to be answered.

When the **ovaries** are encouraged to **superovulate** they can produce up to twelve mature eggs or even more in one **menstrual cycle**. These eggs are **fertilized** and a small number of healthy embryos are then transferred back into the **uterus** of the mother. But this leaves a problem. There may well be other healthy embryos remaining in their dishes. What is to be done with them?

The use of frozen human **sperm** goes back many years. The use of frozen human embryos is much more recent, although animal embryos have been transported around the world in this way for some time. It seems a very dramatic treatment for such delicate tissue, but it appears to cause no damage. Here, frozen embryos are being removed from storage.

Most IVF clinics now offer embryo freezing and storage to their clients. The early embryos are frozen and stored in flasks of liquid nitrogen. This has many advantages. If the first attempt at IVF fails, the couple can have at least one if not more attempts without having to go through the whole process of **fertility drugs** and egg collection again. If, on the other hand, the first attempt is successful, then the remaining embryos can be kept so that, if and when the couple decide they would like another child, they have embryos ready to use. Again this makes the whole process quicker, less traumatic and less expensive for all concerned. However, the presence of these frozen embryos does raise some questions. One of the simplest is – what happens to the embryos once a couple decide their family is complete?

The embryos may simply be destroyed, but this is not the most usual fate for them. If the parents are willing – and they often are – the embryos may be used for further research into the treatment of human fertility. They may be allowed to continue developing until they are fourteen days old – all research on embryos older than that is banned in the UK and many other countries follow the same rule. Another alternative is that one couple may donate their 'spare' embryos to another infertile couple who cannot produce healthy ones. Many other couples decide to keep their frozen embryos 'just in case' – although most clinics put a limit on the number of years they will keep the embryos before disposing of them. This is not a callous gesture – no one knows for sure the effect of long-term freezing on the future health of the children who might grow from the embryos. (For more on this subject, see pages 46–7.)

Zoe Leyland was born in Australia in 1984. She was the first frozen embryo to become a live baby, and seemed to suffer no ill effects from her time in the deep freeze.

Doriver's story

The theory of the causes of **infertility** and the way they can be overcome, including high-tech treatments like IVF, make the whole process sound very neat, orderly and scientific. However, when the science meets the real world all of that neatness goes. Infertility involves real people and the treatments can be messy, take a long time and often don't even work. So what is infertility treatment *really* like?

Doriver and Ian Lilley got married when Doriver was only 20 and they planned to start a family about five years later. 'In fact it was almost six years before I threw away my pills. We were going on holiday and I half-expected to come back pregnant!' explained Doriver. But things didn't go quite as planned – Doriver wasn't pregnant when they came back from holiday and she still wasn't pregnant 18 months later. At this point Ian and Doriver went to see their doctor, but even at this stage they weren't too worried – they weren't desperate about having a family, it was just something that everybody did.

When Ian and Doriver Lilley got married in 1985 they expected to spend a few years enjoying themselves and saving before settling down to family life. But things didn't quite work out …

Because they had already been trying for a baby for some time, and they had a sympathetic doctor, they were referred quite quickly to an infertility specialist. This isn't always the case – some couples wait a long time trying different 'low-tech' methods before they are referred to a specialist. As the investigations got under way it all began to seem more serious. None of the initial tests showed any reason why Doriver and Ian were not getting pregnant, yet nothing they tried actually worked. Even when the doctor suggested that they tried the **fertility drug** Clomid, nothing happened. All of the treatments which sound so effective in theory did not have the desired effect on the reproductive systems of Doriver and Ian.

> 'Every time something fails, infertility becomes harder to deal with, as you begin to realize it might not work – ever.'
>
> Doriver Lilley

Infertility takes over

The infertility began to take over Doriver's life, so she could think of little else. For Ian, 'The hardest part was watching the woman I love suffer so much pain and being unable to do anything about it.'

For both of them, being completely out of control of the situation was an alien and very unpleasant experience. In most areas of life people have at least some level of control over their actions and choices – when infertility strikes, that control is removed. Not conceiving made Doriver feel a total failure, and it was very hard having to rely on other people for such a very intimate and personal thing as having a baby. And so far, science had failed them too.

As Doriver and Ian live in the UK, their treatment up to this point was provided free by the National Health Service (NHS). Several years and a wide variety of treatments passed by without their conceiving a baby, and without any clear reason for their infertility emerging. But they couldn't have any more treatment free – if they wanted to try IVF they would have to pay for it themselves because their NHS doctors felt there was little chance they would succeed in becoming pregnant. By this stage Doriver was feeling desperate.

> 'Everyone else seemed pregnant. I kept going in to work, but it was so hard to keep appearing cheerful. Every day when I got home, I'd break down and cry because I couldn't cope with it...'
>
> Doriver Lilley

Beginning IVF

Making the decision to begin IVF treatment had a strange effect – it lightened the load on their shoulders. The fact that they were trying something different, something very advanced and cutting-edge, gave them a renewed sense of optimism – surely something was going to happen now! Again, in theory, IVF should be a straightforward solution, but where living systems are concerned, science and technology sometimes come unstuck.

Will IVF be the answer?

The IVF programme moved forward rapidly under Dr John Webster. John had been present at the birth of Louise Brown, the first test-tube baby, so Doriver and Ian felt they were in very good hands. However, they knew that if IVF didn't work, there was nothing else left to try. The first treatment was exciting. Doriver's eggs were harvested – in itself an exciting victory – and some healthy **embryos** were formed and transferred back into her body. They even had a very weakly positive pregnancy test, but the embryos did not implant properly, the levels of pregnancy **hormones** dropped and the 'pregnancy' ended just a few days later. In spite of the disappointment Doriver was encouraged, because they *had* got eggs and they *had* got embryos.

The second attempt was a crushing blow. It failed completely. The quality of the embryos was poor – even the two transferred back into Doriver were only two cells and rather fragmented. Ideally the cells making up an embryo are all the same size and have smooth **membranes**. These had rough membranes with pieces breaking off. There was no pregnancy. Things looked black – financially the treatment had left them £6000 poorer and they still didn't have a baby. The more failed IVF treatments a couple have, the less likely they are statistically to ever end up with a successful pregnancy – and Doriver and Ian were well aware of these figures.

> *'I knew that statistically our chances were getting less and less each time we tried – but I also knew that as long as we had any money to spend I was going to keep on trying.'*
>
> Doriver Lilley

Doriver and Ian came into a small amount of money – and immediately enlisted for their third attempt at IVF.

Steve Green is an **embryologist**, one of the team at the CARE clinic at The Park Hospital where Ian and Doriver went for treatment. His role was to make sure that the embryos which were replaced in Doriver's uterus were healthy and growing well.

'There was a huge pressure to provide good quality **sperm**. Doriver had been through so much, everything was ready and waiting, she was in theatre and then it all hinged on my one involvement!'

Ian Lilley

Eggs were harvested, healthy embryos formed and transferred into Doriver's **uterus** – and the waiting began. This time the pregnancy test was strongly positive – at least one embryo had definitely implanted in the uterus wall!

Pregnant at last!

At 32 years old, after six years of trying, Doriver was finally pregnant – but she couldn't believe it! She refused to accept that she really could be pregnant, yet was terrified in case anything went wrong with the pregnancy that she didn't believe was real. She found herself constantly rushing to the toilet, checking to see if her **period** had started, but another six weeks passed with no problems.

> 'After embryo replacement I did everything in the house and got all our meals ready etc. I know that you are told it doesn't make any difference [what you do in your daily life], but after so long we were not going to take that chance.'
>
> Ian Lilley

Still refusing to believe what was happening, Doriver and Ian went for their first **ultrasound** scan, and when it showed not one but two tiny beating hearts, two little embryos growing strongly, they were completely bowled over. Not only were they pregnant, they were expecting twins! By the time Daniel and Jordanne arrived safely, Doriver had just about accepted that she was pregnant. Nevertheless she was still deeply anxious that things would go wrong.

> 'Even when I was in labour, when I went into hospital, I kept thinking "This is it, this is when I'm going to lose them." I just couldn't believe we were really going to have children of our own.'
>
> Doriver Lilley

> 'When I saw my son being born and I could see his face start to emerge I couldn't believe I was finally to meet my children after so long.'
>
> Ian Lilley

After the twins were born Doriver had little time to marvel at how they had arrived. Caring for newborn twins is enormously time-consuming and tiring – but this was what all the trying and waiting had been about. During infertility treatment the focus is on getting pregnant – it can be easy to forget that at the end of a pregnancy there are babies that grow up into children to look after.

Fate had one more twist in the tale, because just when Doriver was planning to return to work she found she was pregnant again, without any artificial intervention. Doriver and Ian were shocked – once again the unpredictability of human **fertility** had thrown their carefully made plans into disarray. Science has definite limitations – it had been unable to explain their infertility, even though it had eventually enabled them to overcome it, and now science could not really explain their new-found fertility. But once they had got over the shock, there was excitement all round when James made his entry into the world. From childlessness four years ago, Doriver and Ian are now the happy, proud, exhausted and somewhat bemused parents of three lovely, healthy children – and a glowing advertisement for what IVF can achieve. The years of research that went into the development of IVF technology have brought happy endings like this for thousands of couples in the UK, USA, Australia, Europe and other parts of the world.

Doriver with Daniel, Jordanne and their little brother James. As these children grow up, there will be no way of telling that two of them would not exist if it weren't for IVF technology.

Beyond IVF

The techniques of IVF are constantly being refined and adjusted to find ways of giving the highest possible chance of success to **infertile** couples. For example, for many years **embryos** have been transferred at the four- or eight-cell stage. Recent work suggests that transferring the **blastocysts** (five-day-old embryos) will give better pregnancy rates, because this is the stage at which the embryo would enter the **uterus** in a natural **conception**.

However, there have also been a number of other new technologies developed that help to overcome even more infertility problems. Most of these also involve embryo transfer.

Donor eggs

One of the ways in which IVF has moved forward is in the use of **donor** eggs. It has been shown that if a couple are having trouble conceiving and the woman is over 40, it may be necessary to use an egg donor to achieve a successful pregnancy. In couples with this problem IVF has been shown to be much more successful when the eggs of a younger women – less than 37 years old – who is already known to be **fertile** herself are used. It is not just in couples where the woman at least is older that donor eggs are very useful. Women who have no eggs in their **ovaries** cannot become pregnant without an egg donor. Also women who carry a **genetic** disease may need to use donor eggs to avoid passing on a debilitating illness. So the use of donor eggs in IVF, along with donor embryos mentioned earlier, has increased the success rate for older women.

> 'Fertility in women is known to decline with age, strikingly so after 35, and reproductive capacity is all but lost by the age of 45.'
>
> Mr Andrew Kan and Mr Hossam Abdulla, IVF specialists, Lister Hospital

Some doctors use this technology to allow women who are well over the natural age for childbearing to have children. Naturally, a woman passes through the menopause at between 45 and 55 years. At this point she no longer has **periods** and her ovaries became inactive – no more eggs are released. But by using donor eggs or embryos, women over the age of 50 have been enabled to give birth.

In 1994, Rosanna della Corte, an Italian woman, gave birth to a baby boy when she was 62. Artificial **hormones** had been used to prepare her uterus, and once the pregnancy was established her body took over and maintained the pregnancy just like a younger woman.

Since the initial breakthrough more than 100 women aged 50 or over have had babies in the USA alone. However, only relatively few clinics will treat older women in this way. There are many people who have real concerns about it, both because of the potential risks to the health of the mother and the age gap between the mother and child – although similar arguments are rarely put forward when older men father children naturally!

'When that child is of college age, his mother will be 80. That is, if she is still alive. We're designing orphans by choice, and we say this is OK?'
John Paris, professor of **bioethics** at Boston College and a Jesuit priest, speaking of Rosanna della Corte's offspring

GIFT – another alternative

GIFT stands for Gamete Intra Fallopian Transfer. It is a modified version of IVF that involves harvesting the eggs and placing them and the **sperm** into a healthy **Fallopian tube**. The idea is that **fertilization** then takes place within the natural environment of the body instead of in a glass dish, and any embryos which form will then travel down the remaining part of the Fallopian tube to the uterus where they will implant as normal. GIFT has a similar success rate to IVF. However, because it involves surgery (a **laparoscopy**) most UK clinics prefer to use IVF.

Injecting sperm – a major breakthrough

Until recently there was no help for couples where the male partner did not produce fertile sperm, apart from **artificial insemination** by a donor. Recent developments have changed all that, and there are now techniques available which mean it is possible, in theory at least, for almost any man to father a child.

The main technique used is known as **ICSI**. This stands for Intra Cytoplasmic Sperm Injection. Eggs are harvested from a woman after treatment with **fertility drugs** in the same way as for IVF. A single sperm is then injected into the **cytoplasm** of each egg cell. The fertilized eggs are then observed as they divide to form early embryos.

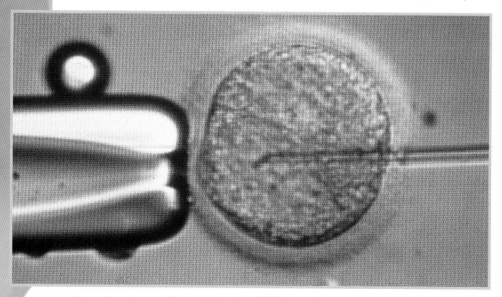

Intra Cytoplasmic Sperm Injection (ICSI) involves using a needle to inject a single sperm right into the centre of an egg cell so that fertilization can take place. This removes all the normal barriers to conception as the sperm cannot fail to reach the egg.

Two or three healthy embryos will then be returned to the body of the mother just as in normal IVF treatment.

> 'ICSI technology has revolutionized the treatment of male factor infertility. This is considerable, because we now appreciate that male factor infertility is probably the single largest cause of infertility amongst couples.'
>
> Dr Simon Fischel, CARE clinic, The Park Hospital

The first baby to be born using ICSI was born in 1992. In 1993, there were three clinics in the UK carrying out this procedure; by 1997, there were 43 clinics in the UK alone offering ICSI, and the numbers are still growing. In the USA, Australia and Europe too, the value of ICSI was quickly recognized. In fact ICSI is now chosen as the best treatment for at least 30 per cent of all the couples who need IVF technology.

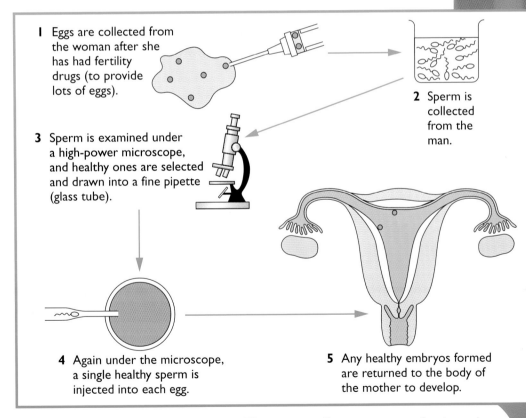

1 Eggs are collected from the woman after she has had fertility drugs (to provide lots of eggs).

2 Sperm is collected from the man.

3 Sperm is examined under a high-power microscope, and healthy ones are selected and drawn into a fine pipette (glass tube).

4 Again under the microscope, a single healthy sperm is injected into each egg.

5 Any healthy embryos formed are returned to the body of the mother to develop.

These are the steps in the ICSI procedure. This process offers two groups of patients the hope of a successful pregnancy: firstly, men who have very few healthy sperm or who cannot produce **semen** at all, as it only takes one sperm to fertilize each egg; secondly, couples who produce healthy eggs and sperm for IVF but cannot achieve fertilization – this can be overcome by the direct insertion of a sperm into an egg.

Ethics, issues and the law

The new reproductive technologies from IVF onwards have brought great happiness and benefit to thousands of couples who have been enabled to have children – over 50,000 children in the UK alone. However, they have also raised many different issues that people as individuals and society as a whole need to consider. Some of the issues are very practical, and are the direct result of IVF technology.

> 'When making decisions about **infertility** treatment you have to consider the MEEF equation:
> Medical issues + Ethical issues + Emotional issues + Financial issues = Treatment.'
>
> Mr Michael Dooley, consultant, Winterbourne Hospital Infertility Clinic

Money matters

One important issue is that of cost. IVF treatment is expensive. In both the UK and Australia the state pays for a certain amount of infertility treatment. In the UK, that sometimes includes a limited number of attempts at IVF. In Australia, until recently, there was a limit of six attempts, but that has recently been lifted. However, there is an issue about whether it is right for large amounts of state money to be used to enable a few infertile couples to have children, when there is a shortage of money for other medical treatments that may be life-threatening. In the USA the situation is very different – everyone has to pay for their treatment. However, medical insurance has often refused to foot the bill for infertility treatment, claiming that infertility is not an illness. Increasingly, individual states are bringing in legislation that forces medical insurance companies to cover infertility treatment, including IVF and **ICSI**, making help available to many more couples than before.

Frozen embryos

If a treatment cycle results in more healthy **embryos** than can be safely transferred into the woman, then those embryos are often frozen for possible later use. If the parents of those embryos later divorce, who do the embryos belong to? This is an important issue, because ultimately the parents of the embryos decide what is to become of them, and if the couple are divorced and do not agree about the fate of the embryos, who then takes responsibility for them? Another scenario that must be considered is that of both parents dying in an accident before they have successfully had children. If there are still healthy frozen embryos, should they be implanted inside a **surrogate mother** and brought into the world to inherit their parents' belongings?

In all of these debates the welfare of the potential children has to be paramount. It could be extremely damaging for children to feel that they had been pawns in their parents' divorce settlement or brought into being to make sure money stayed in the family.

In theory, frozen embryos could be kept for around 10,000 years before the natural background radiation of the Earth damaged their **DNA** to the extent that they would not grow and develop properly. In practice, after a certain amount of time most couples decide either to use the embryos themselves, donate them to another couple or allow them to be used for research.

In the UK there are legal limits – frozen embryos can only be kept for five years, with another five years' extension possible if the parents need more time to decide if they want to add to their family. This gives a total of ten years of embryo storage. As no one knows for certain how long frozen embryos can be stored safely, this limit attempts to protect children who might be born damaged in some way from eggs stored for longer than ten years. Other countries have less strict laws and regulations about limits. This again raises child welfare issues, making it possible for one sibling to be 30 or even 40 years younger than the other. But whatever the legal situation, the existence of frozen embryos raises difficult issues.

> '*Initially the embryos just offered me an option, another chance of having a baby, but we'd lost so many embryos they didn't really mean a lot. But once I'd had Daniel and Jordanne, part of me had a sentimental vision of these tiny babies frozen. I had given the twins their chance of life, shouldn't I do the same for the frozen embryos? And then the logical part of me says that they are collections of four cells, and that it would be better to give them to someone else or let them be used for research. It's really difficult...*'
>
> Doriver Lilley

Embryo research

The use of embryos for research is another very sensitive issue. Without embryo research, infertility treatment would never have reached the point it has today. Further steps forward, widening the net of people who can be helped to have a child, depend on more research. Yet this research is carried out on tiny clusters of cells, some of which might, if transferred into a woman's body, turn into babies. For some this is very difficult to accept, and there are groups of people in every country in which this type of research is carried out who object to it very strongly.

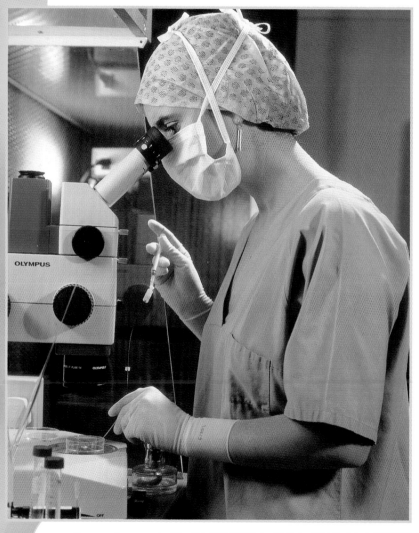

Research on embryos raises people's emotions, whether they are for or against it. But while it is legal the research will continue, and infertile couples and couples with **genetic** diseases will benefit from the results.

Surrogate mothers

The ability to **fertilize** eggs outside of the body has paved the way for another controversial form of infertility treatment – the use of a surrogate mother. Some women have **ovaries** that work perfectly well but do not have a **uterus**, whilst other women have no reproductive organs at all. Their only chance of having a baby apart from adoption is if another woman will carry a baby for them. This might involve IVF, with embryos from one couple transferred into the uterus of another woman or it might involve **artificial insemination** of the surrogate mother with **sperm** from the father. Whatever the method, the baby grows and develops inside the surrogate mother, who then hands the baby over to its parents very shortly after birth.

There are all sorts of problems with surrogacy. In the USA it is legal and is carried out for money by a number of very successful businesses. In the UK and Australia it is legal but there can be no payment given to a woman for carrying another person's child. The biggest problem is if the surrogate mother decides she cannot hand over the child. There have been legal battles between biological and surrogate parents – and in the first test case in the USA, the 'purchasing' parents were granted custody of the child, whilst the surrogate mother was granted visiting rights.

There have been a surprising number of successful surrogate relationships, including ones where a sister has carried a baby for her sibling who is unable to have children, as shown here. Many surrogates are very happy mothers themselves who feel they are giving someone else the gift of a child.

49

The law

With the arrival of new technologies there have been legal problems. When dealing with potential human life the risks are great, and different countries have set about dealing with them in different ways. The first concern in most legislation is the welfare of any potential children born using new technology. If there is concern that the health or well-being of the babies conceived might be affected by the technology then most countries are unhappy about its use.

IVF began in the UK, and the UK responded to this giant step forward with a regulatory body known as the Human Fertilisation and Embryology Authority or HFEA. Set up in 1991, the HFEA makes sure that all clinics offering IVF and other infertility treatments in the UK meet strict standards. They collect information about success rates, and provide information to the public. The HFEA also licence and monitor

When people wish to change the law they often stage a protest, like these people here. Attempts to change national law in Australia to allow states to ban IVF for single people sparked off such protests.

all embryo research, supervising what is going on and balancing what should and should not be done. Decisions are made by the 21 members of the authority, who are experts in relevant fields. To make sure that a wide spectrum of views are heard, more than half of the team are not involved in medicine or human embryo research.

> 'The first IVF baby was born in the UK and we were the first **statutory** government body to regulate this treatment and remain one of the few to do so. While the number of couples seeking IVF treatment rapidly increases we aim to assure a high standard of care and medical expertise whether that clinic is private or public, big or small.'
>
> Ruth Deech, HFEA chairman

So in the UK, things are relatively straightforward. If a treatment is allowed by the HFEA it goes ahead, if it is not it doesn't.

In other countries things are not so clear-cut. In both the USA and Australia there are two layers of legislation. There is central national legislation and then legislation at state level. This can cause problems and confusion. For example, in Australia one state wanted to prevent single people from receiving IVF treatment. This caused an uproar in the gay community, because two people of the same sex cannot legally marry in Australia. This means any gay person wanting to have a child is legally single and so would be unable to have fertility treatment. In response to the outcry, national law was used to stop the state law. There have since been moves to try and change the national law to allow states to make their own decisions. A solution has yet to be found.

In the USA there is a similarly fragmented situation. There are few laws controlling what techniques or research may or may not be carried out. However, legislation compelling medical insurance companies to pay for IVF treatment is being introduced in an increasing number of states, making IVF and other treatments available to more and more couples in the USA.

In most US clinics, doctors work to the same high scientific, medical and ethical standards expected from doctors all around the world. However, it is easier for less scrupulous doctors and researchers to experiment or carry out less ethical treatments if there is no legislation to prevent them from doing so.

A matter of faith

The decisions a couple make about infertility treatments may be affected by their religious beliefs. There is no single view within the different faiths about the acceptability or otherwise of infertility treatments such as IVF. This means that one couple may undergo IVF sure in the belief that it is acceptable, whilst another couple, equally desperate to have a child, may feel unable to accept IVF.

The Anglican view

The views of the Anglican Church have strong foundations in a belief in marriage and the family and in respect for human life. Therefore the Church does not object in principle to fertility treatment that involves reopening the **Fallopian tubes** or the use of **fertility drugs**. Artificial insemination with the husband's sperm is also seen as universally acceptable. However, IVF itself raises more of an issue for some theologians, who see it as a way of improving on nature rather than helping it and therefore as an attempt to 'play God'. Many other Anglican theologians see the process as a perfectly acceptable way of enabling married couples to enter into the blessing of family life.

The Anglican Church is more concerned about the use of donated eggs, sperm or embryos, because it can be argued that by bringing a third party into the relationship the marriage vows are broken. The most liberal view accepts any fertility treatment carried out with due reverence and faith, whilst the most conservative view is that any intervention such as IVF is wrong.

The Catholic standpoint

The teaching of the Catholic Church on infertility treatments is strict and is the same in every country. In 1987 the Pope made the Catholic position very clear in a document called *Donum vitae* ('Respect for life'). He said that treatments such as IVF are not acceptable because they separate the **conception** of a child from the sexual act between the parents. The Catholic Church also rejects completely any infertility treatment that involves donated eggs, sperm or embryos as gravely immoral because of the introduction of another person into the marriage bond.

A Muslim perspective

Within Islam the production of children is a vitally important part of married life. Islam teaching also states that for every illness there is a cure, so it is regarded as acceptable and right that an infertile couple should seek help. Treatments such as fertility drugs and procedures to open up the Fallopian tubes are quite acceptable. Islamic scholars also

For many people the spiritual dimension of their lives – their religion – is important in guiding their decisions about fertility treatments.

accept the use of IVF, but only if enormous care is taken that only the eggs and sperm of the husband and wife concerned are used in the treatment. But, as in many other religions, the use of donated eggs, sperm or embryos is seen as completely unacceptable because it breaks the unity of the marriage bond.

The Jewish approach

As in so many other religions, the family is very important to the Jewish faith. Orthodox Jewish law finds assisted **reproduction** acceptable in helping a Jewish couple to conceive a child as long as the eggs and sperm come from the parents themselves. So IVF using sex cells from the parents is acceptable, and there is often a **rabbinical** supervisor present to make sure that the eggs and sperm are not contaminated by material from non-Jews. But the use of **donor** eggs or sperm is much less acceptable, and certainly not allowed if the sex cells are not from Jewish people.

The Hindu approach

For Hindus, with their beliefs in reincarnation and caste (inherited social status), treatments such as IVF raise many problems. Only a husband is allowed to touch his wife, so a doctor cannot intervene in the act of conception, and fear of caste contamination makes donor eggs and sperm unacceptable to strict Hindus.

Where do we go from here?

One of the most exciting developments in IVF technology is the ability to help overcome **genetic** diseases. In some families there are errors in the genetic code that result in incurable diseases which can be fatal. In Tay Sachs disease, which mainly affects Jewish families, the nervous system of the child gradually breaks down and they die before reaching five years of age. Huntington's disease affects people in their forties or fifties, causing irreversible damage in the brain followed by death. Another disease, cystic fibrosis, causes the cells of all the tubes in the body to produce a thick, sticky **mucus** which blocks the tubes and allows massive infections to build up. It shortens life expectancy considerably.

Down's syndrome is one of many inherited genetic disorders. For some families with these conditions, genetic screening and IVF offer ways of ensuring that their children are free from the disease. However, some couples feel they cannot use these methods because it is against their faith.

For couples who know they may carry these diseases, the decision to have a family is fraught with despair, because it involves a genetic lottery. While all their children may be born healthy, if they are unlucky they will all suffer from the genetic disease. However, IVF technology combined with methods developed for **genetic engineering** offers a way forward. In some specialized clinics couples carrying genetic diseases can be helped to have healthy children. Some genetic diseases such as haemophilia (in which the blood does not clot properly) and Duchenne muscular dystrophy (in which the muscles deteriorate until the child dies) only affect boys. They are known as sex-linked diseases. If a couple plan to have a baby using IVF, a single cell from each developing **embryo** can be extracted and its sex determined – girls have two X **chromosomes** in the **nucleus** of their cells, whilst boys have an X and a Y. When there is a risk of sex-linked disease, only female embryos will be transferred to the mother, so a daughter free from the genetic disease is guaranteed.

Over the last few years we have built up a much better understanding of the whole of the human genetic material (known as the human genome) including many individual genes. As a result it is becoming increasingly possible to identify embryos that carry disease-causing genes.

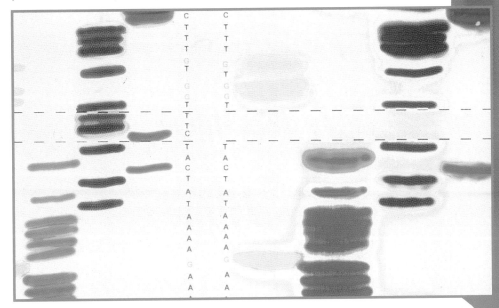

In a complex procedure that only takes place at a few clinics at the moment, one cell is removed from the embryo. Using technology developed for genetic engineering, the **DNA** from the cell is duplicated many times over. With such a large sample, individual faulty genes can be picked out by comparing them with known DNA profiles using the comparison technique shown above. Only healthy embryos are then transferred to the mother's body.

Cloning

Cloning mammals involves making an identical copy of an adult animal. This has been done a number of times with animals such as sheep.

Dolly the sheep was cloned from the adult cell of another sheep. The nucleus of an adult udder cell was placed in an egg cell and then transferred to the uterus of the '**surrogate mother**'. Scientists are still investigating Dolly, but she has proved her normality by giving birth naturally to a lamb of her own.

People are now wondering if and when the cloning of people will take place. IVF would make it possible, because the cloned cell would have to be transferred to a **uterus** to grow and develop into a baby, but many people are suspicious of the idea. There are worries that rich and famous people might try to clone themselves to become immortal, or that another Adolf Hitler might try to use such technology along with genetic engineering to produce a 'master race' of people. In some countries it is illegal to attempt to clone a human being, but in others some scientists are already planning to try and produce the first human clone. They feel it will help overcome the problem of **infertility** – if an infertile woman can give birth to a clone of her partner or herself it would remove the need to use **donor sperm** or eggs, which can be in short supply and cause religious problems.

Into the future

The future of infertility treatments looks bright. The techniques are being refined and improved all the time, and the numbers of people who have a child through IVF or related treatments continue to grow. Hundreds of thousands of IVF babies are alive today, children who would not exist without the miracle of ground-breaking scientific techniques that allow eggs to be **fertilized** outside of their mother's body. The benefits to the individuals concerned are immeasurable and society benefits too from the birth of more children free from genetic diseases.

However, there are two sides to every story and many people are questioning the acceptability of some of the treatments now being suggested, such as cloning and the use of spare embryos for the development of medical treatments. But the clock cannot be turned back, we cannot return to the situation before these treatments were discovered, nor would most people wish to do so. The development of IVF and other treatments will continue for the foreseeable future, fulfilling an ever-growing demand, and the debate within society will continue alongside it.

Louise Brown, the very first 'test-tube baby', is now a young woman in her own right. Here she holds two of the hundreds of thousands of IVF babies that have joined her since those early, groundbreaking days in 1978!

Timeline

AD200 Records show Jewish thinkers discussing the possibility of accidental or unintentional **artificial insemination**.

1300s There are accounts of Arabs using artificial insemination on horses.

1777 Italian priest begins experiments with the artificial insemination of reptiles.

1785 First attempts at human artificial insemination by John Hunter, a Scottish surgeon – a baby is born the same year as a result.

1890 In the UK, Robert Dickinson begins experimenting with **donor sperm**, although his work is carried out in secret because of the condemnation of the Church.

1945 Early reports of artificial insemination using donor sperm published in the *British Medical Journal*.

1949 Dr Piero Donini, an Italian, produces the first human **fertility drug**.

1954 Four successful pregnancies take place using previously frozen sperm.

1960s Big increase in understanding of the female reproductive system and the process of **fertilization**. Drugs are developed that stimulate **ovaries** so they produce eggs, and **laparoscopy** methods are improved, making the treatment safer.

1962 First baby born as a result of drug-triggered **ovulation**.

1969 Human fertilization *in vitro* is achieved for the first time.

1975   First IVF pregnancy occurs, but it is **ectopic**.

1978   Birth of Louise Brown, the first 'test-tube' baby
        born as a result of IVF.

1980   Two Australian teams succeed in IVF
        deliveries after drug-induced **superovulation**
        in the mother.

1984   The Warnock Report in the UK calls for a **statutory** body
        to control reproductive technology.

1988–9 **GIFT** introduced and the first successful
        pregnancies achieved.

1990   Human Fertilisation and Embryology Act in the UK followed
        by the setting up of the Human Fertilisation and Embryology
        Authority (HFEA) in 1991.

1992   First baby born as a result of **ICSI**.

1994   At the age of 62, Rosanna della Corte gives birth to a son,
        after IVF treatment.

1996   The birth of Dolly the sheep, the first cloned mammal.

1998   Growing embryonic **stem cells** in the laboratory opens the
        way for different types of cells and organs to be grown as
        needed for use in transplant surgery. Some of these stem
        cells come from 'spare' embryos donated by a couple who
        have had successful IVF treatment.

2001   Teams in the USA and Italy announce that they are working
        on producing the first human clone.

        A French woman of 62 who wants a child to inherit her
        property and money has a baby through IVF, using sperm
        from her brother and a donated egg.

Glossary

artificial insemination inserting sperm into the vagina using a device, rather than through sexual intercourse

bioethics the moral rights and wrongs of situations linked to biological advances

blastocyst hollow ball of cells formed after the fertilization of an egg

cervix lower part of the uterus that extends into the vagina

chromosome one of the thread-like structures in a nucleus, made up of DNA and protein. Each chromosome carries many different genes.

circumvent to get round

conception fertilization of an egg by a sperm, followed by the egg's implantation in the wall of the uterus

contraception using a condom, contraceptive pill or other method to prevent the conception of a child

cytoplasm jelly-like substance which fills the cell and in which the components of the cell are suspended

DNA (deoxyribonucleic acid) type of nucleic acid, found in the nucleus of a cell, which carries the genetic code

donor someone who gives an organ or a product of their body – for example eggs or sperm – to help someone who has a faulty organ or product

ectopic pregnancy pregnancy in which the embryo implants and develops in one of the Fallopian tubes instead of in the uterus

embryo term for an egg after it has been fertilized, when it is in its early stages of development

embryologist doctor or scientist who specializes in the study of embryos

enzyme special protein that makes possible or speeds up the rate of chemical reactions

ethics consideration of what is morally right or wrong

Fallopian tube one of a pair of tubes that link the ovaries and the uterus in the female reproductive system

fertility, fertile ability to produce offspring

fertility drugs chemicals that stimulate the development of mature eggs in the follicles of the ovary

fertilization union of egg and sperm that is necessary to produce offspring

follicle cell surrounding the developing egg in the ovary

Follicle Stimulating Hormone (FSH) sex hormone which causes some of the follicles of the ovary to ripen and the eggs within them to mature

genetic to do with the genes, the units of inheritance that are passed on from parent to offspring and determine the offspring's characteristics. Each gene is made from a length of DNA, found in the nucleus of a cell.

genetic engineering process by which the genetic material of a cell may be altered either by replacing damaged genetic material or adding extra genetic material

GIFT Gamete Intra Fallopian Transfer, a modified version of IVF which involves harvesting the eggs and mixing them with sperm before replacing them inside the Fallopian tube

gynaecologist doctor who specializes in problems of the female reproductive system

hormone chemical messenger made in one place in the body which has an effect somewhere else in the body

ICSI Intra Cytoplasmic Sperm Injection, the injection of a single sperm right into the cytoplasm of each egg cell

in vitro Latin for 'in glass' – term used to describe the fertilization of an egg in a Petri dish

infertility, infertile inability to produce offspring

laparoscopy technique for looking at the Fallopian tubes by inserting an instrument into the abdomen

membrane thin, skin-like tissue covering organs and cells

menstrual cycle approximately 28-day cycle of female fertility

mucus slimy substance produced by membranes in some parts of the body

nucleus (plural = nuclei) central part of a cell, which controls many cell functions and contains a person's DNA

oestrogen female sex hormone made by the ovaries, involved in the release of a mature egg

ovaries pair of female sex organs where eggs are stored and mature, and where the sex hormones oestrogen and progesterone are produced

ovulation release of a mature egg from the ovary

ovum (egg) female sex cell

period time (usually lasting 5–7 days) in the middle of the menstrual cycle when pregnancy has not occurred and when the lining of the uterus is shed resulting in bleeding. Also called menstruation.

Petri dish small shallow dish made from thin glass, traditionally used for studying the behaviour of bacteria

physiologist someone who studies the human body and its functions

pituitary gland small structure in the brain which produces many hormones

progesterone hormone of pregnancy which prevents menstruation from occurring

pros and cons reasons for and against something

puberty stage when the body of a child undergoes physical development to become a sexually mature adult

rabbinical concerned with Jewish law

reproduction the making of a new individual

semen mixture of sperm and fluids produced by a man when he ejaculates (discharges semen)

sperm male sex cell

statutory having legal authority

stem cells 'immortal' cell that retains the ability to divide and multiply and to create other types of cell. Stem cells are found in embryos, bone marrow, skin, intestine and muscle tissue.

superovulate when women produce many mature follicles containing mature eggs ready for release at the same time

surrogate mother woman who carries a baby for a couple who are unable to have a child of their own

testes pair of male sex organs in which sperm and semen are produced along with the male sex hormone testosterone

ultrasound using extremely high frequency sound waves to produce images of inside the human body. Used for examining developing babies in the womb.

uterus organ of the female reproductive system in which the baby grows and develops (also known as the womb)

Sources of information

Further reading

Collins Advanced Science: Human Biology, Mike Boyle and Bill Indge (Collins, 1999)

Science Topics: The Human Body, Ann Fullick (Heinemann Library, 1998)

Let's Talk about Sex, Robie H. Harris (Walker Books, 1994)

Biology Now!, Peter D. Riley (John Murray, 1998)

Websites

The following websites give information on different types of infertility treatment, on the history of reproductive medicine and how to find the right fertility treatment:

www.ferti.net (Worldwide Fertility Network)

Provides information on fertility and treatment, with a library of articles and links to other sites.

www.infertility-info.com (Information site on Assisted Reproduction)

Features assisted reproduction techniques, answers to frequently asked questions and gives access to the WEBROM library.

www.repromed.co.uk (Centre for Reproductive Medicine, Bristol, UK)

Gives information on reproductive medicine, specifically fertility, menopause and support groups. Also provides details of Bristol University's Centre for Reproductive Medicine which was established in 1983; the centre has both research and clinical involvement in IVF treatment.

Author sources

The following materials were used by the author in the writing of this book:

Hormones in Reproduction, C.R. Austin and R.V. Short (Cambridge University Press, 1972)

Heinemann Advanced Science: Biology, Ann Fullick (Heinemann Educational, 2000)

Human Health and Disease, Ann Fullick (Heinemann Educational, 1998)

Family Experience of Multiple Births from Fertility Treatment: The Value of Person-to-Person Support, N.J. Monks, M.D. Dooley, L. Wallace and C. McDonough (Archives of Perinatal Medicine)

Factsheets produced by Child, the National Infertility Support Network in the UK

Index

artificial insemination 18, 19, 44, 49, 52

blastocysts 20, 21, 42
Brown, Louise 23, 39, 57

cervix 8, 14, 29
child welfare issues 47, 50
cloning 56, 57
conception 13, 16, 42, 52
contraception 5, 11
counselling 24

DNA 20, 47, 55
donor eggs 13, 33, 42–3, 52, 53, 56
donor embryos 35, 42, 52, 53
donor sperm 15, 19, 52, 53, 56
dye tests 14

ectopic pregnancy 22
Edwards, Dr Robert 21, 22, 23, 24
eggs (ova) 4, 6, 7, 8, 9, 12–13, 16–17, 20, 21, 22, 24, 26-8
  donor eggs 13, 33, 42–3, 52, 53, 56
  harvesting 16, 21, 22, 27, 44, 45
embryos 5, 20, 22, 24, 28–9, 33–4, 39, 42, 44, 45, 55
  donor embryos 35, 42, 52, 53
  embryo research 35, 47, 48, 50, 57
  frozen embryos 34–5, 46–7
ethics 5, 46–9

Fallopian tubes 7, 8, 9, 13–14, 20, 22, 24, 44, 52, 53
fertility 6, 10, 11, 18, 42
fertility drugs 16, 17, 19, 20, 24, 26, 37, 45, 52

fertilization 4, 9, 13, 18, 20, 28, 34, 44, 49, 57
Follicle Stimulating Hormone (FSH) 7, 13, 16
follicles 21, 26, 27
funding infertility treatment 25, 37, 46, 51

genetic diseases 28, 42, 48, 54–5, 57
genetic engineering 55, 56
genetics 9, 20
GIFT (Gemete Intra Fallopian Transfer) 44

hormones 6–7, 13, 16, 19, 26, 27, 29, 39
Human Fertilisation and Embryology Authority (HFEA) 34, 50, 51
hysterosalpingogram 13, 14

ICSI (Intra Cytoplasmic Sperm Injection) 45, 46
implantation 9, 20, 29, 44
in vitro fertilization (IVF) 5, 11, 16, 18-35, 38–40, 46, 49, 50, 52, 53, 56
  background to 18–20
  case history 36–41
  embryo transfer 29, 42
  failed treatments 39
  first instance of 21
  process 24–5, 26–9, 31
  success rates 32
infertility 5, 10–15, 18, 37
infertility clinics 25, 32-3, 34, 50, 51

laparoscopy 14, 21, 22, 44
legal issues 47, 49, 50-1

lifestyle factors 10, 15, 16

menstrual cycle 6, 8, 26, 34
menstruation 7
multiple pregnancies 17, 24, 31, 33–4

new technologies 42–5

oestrogen 7
older women 33, 42–3
ovaries 6, 7, 12, 16, 19, 21, 26, 34, 42, 43, 49
ovulation 7, 8, 12, 13, 19, 22, 29

periods 30, 40, 43
pituitary gland 7, 19
pregnancy tests 30, 39
progesterone 29

religious issues 52–3
reproduction 6, 18, 20

semen 7, 8, 14–15, 28
sperm 4, 5, 7, 8, 9, 13, 14, 15, 24, 28, 39, 44
  donor sperm 15, 19, 52, 53, 56
  frozen sperm 19, 34
  injecting 5, 15, 44–5
  sperm count 15
Steptoe, Patrick 21, 22, 23, 24
superovulation 24, 34
surrogate mothers 47, 49, 56

'test-tube babies' 23
testes 7, 15, 19

ultrasound scans 26, 30, 40
uterus 7, 8, 9, 13, 17, 20, 24, 29, 34, 42, 49, 56

Titles in the *Science at the Edge* series:

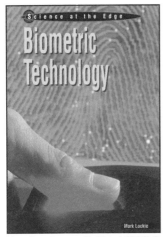

Hardback   0 431 14885 6

Hardback   0 431 14882 1

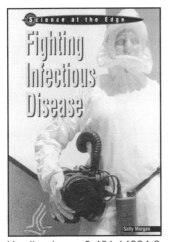

Hardback   0 431 14884 8

Hardback   0 431 14883 X

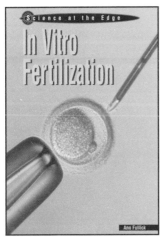

Hardback   0 431 14881 3

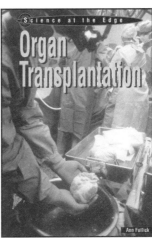

Hardback   0 431 14880 5

Find out about other Heinemann Library titles on our website www.heinemann.co.uk/library